Cajun Keto Recipes

Vonnie Lynn

DEDICATION

This compilation of recipes was written in memory of my husband's incredible grandmother, who was affectionately known as Gram Winnie by those privileged enough to get to taste her cooking. She LOVED to cook. Growing up, my husband and the rest of his family were all well-fed and well-prayed for because of this wonderful woman, and once I joined the family she took me under her wings, too. She is very much missed.

CONTENTS

Other Books By Vonnie Lynn

The Ultimate Keto Diet for Beginners: Keto That Fits Your Lifestyle

And coming soon:
The Ultimate Keto Diet Journal

1 THE KETO BASICS

What is Keto?

The Keto diet is designed to put your body in "ketosis" in order to help you lose weight more quickly. Keto diets cut back on many carbs, especially bad carbs with simple sugars. Unlike the Atkins diet, people on the Keto diet also tend to watch other "macros" instead of just carbohydrates. On a strict Keto diet, even the number of proteins and fats are limited. Also unlike the Atkins diet, Keto maintains a lower number of carbs instead of slowly reintroducing them.

It is important to consult your doctor before starting any diet. In some cases, your doctor may tell you to go on a Keto diet before you approach him or her. It is important to follow the diet plan he or she creates for you.

Ketosis and Ketoacidosis

Ketosis is when your body has run out of carbohydrate fuel and your body begins to convert protein and fats into energy. If you greatly reduce the number of carbohydrates you are taking in each day, you should enter ketosis (the fat burning stage of the diet) in about 3 or 4 days. Some people like to buy breath or blood monitors to check their ketone levels, but these are not necessary for the diet and sometimes checking these numbers all the time can give confusing or mixed results (i.e. checking with a breath meter and then immediately checking with a blood meter may give different numbers).

Although the goal of a Keto diet is to enter ketosis so your body produces ketones, sometimes you can produce too many ketones. This leads to a very dangerous condition called ketoacidosis. Ketoacidosis can occur on the Keto diet or any other low-carbohydrate/ high-fat diet. Certain things, like breastfeeding or drinking alcohol, can aggravate the situation. Symptoms of this serious condition are: excessive urination and thirst, fruity breath, nausea and vomiting, abdominal pain, fluttering heart and/or shortness of breath, confusion, weakness or fatigue. You should seek medical help immediately if you experience these symptoms.

Keto Side Effects

It is important to know that you might have some minor side effects on the Keto diet. Constipation and indigestion seem to be especially prevalent as your body adjusts to it. You may develop insomnia. Some people experience "Keto flu" and become grumpy, tired, and weak. They also might develop bad or fruity breath as well as frequent or prolonged headaches. Occasionally, low-carb diets lead to kidney stones, so it is very important to stay hydrated. Another important thing is to keep track of your blood sugar, which sometimes drops. People who already have health problems may cause these problems to become much worse. This is why it is important to diet under the supervision of a doctor.

Keto Hydration

As your body goes into ketosis, you will naturally start to feel more thirsty. Some people have learned to avoid this feeling and others confuse the feeling of thirst with the feeling of hunger—they may reach for a snack instead of a glass of water. As you continue on the diet, your body will also stop retaining as much water as it needs. Because you are keeping your blood slightly imbalanced with excess ketones, you might also begin to lose needed electrolytes. Needless to say, dehydration is a serious condition. If you notice your urine getting darker, you should begin drinking more water. You might want to consider keeping water in the refrigerator in a measuring pitcher and keeping track of exactly how much you drink each day. Some people drink bullion as a supplement to their meals to improve electrolyte balance.

If your urine becomes extremely dark and you begin to get dizzy or light-headed, you should see a doctor right away. You may need to have intravenous fluids to restore your hydration and electrolyte balance.

Keto is a proven method for losing weight quickly and reducing seizures in epilepsy patients, but like any tool it must be used wisely. This book allows you to maintain your Keto diet while eating some of the traditional Cajun foods you love.

The Good and the Bad (Foods to Eat and those to Avoid)

THE GOOD	THE BAD
Unprocessed, natural meats	Processed meat
Fish and seafood	Breaded fish and fish sticks
Eggs	
Natural fat sauces like butter and coconut fats	Sauces high in carbohydrates and simple sugars like jelly and ketchup.
Green leafy vegetables that grow above the ground such as avocado, Brussels sprouts, and cauliflower.	Root vegetables, which tend to store starchy sugars and are high in carbohydrates.
Dairy foods that are high in fat such as heavy cream and high-fat cheese. Keep in mind these have some carbohydrates in them.	Low-fat yogurt and milk. Dairy contains more carbohydrates when it has less fat.
Low carb nuts like pecans, almonds, and macadamia nuts.	High carb nuts like cashews and pistachios.
Occasional raspberries, strawberries and black berries. These fruits are high in fiber.	Blueberries and fruits like apples or pears that contain a high amount of fiber but many more carbohydrates.

2 BREAKFASTS

Cajun English Muffins

Servings: 6; Net Carbs: 2 g per serving; Calories: 195; Fat: 19 g; Protein: 5 g

- ✓ 3/4 cup almond flour
- ✓ 1/2 cup flaxseed meal
- ✓ 1/4 teaspoon baking soda
- ✓ 1/2 teaspoon baking powder
- ✓ 1/8 teaspoon salt
- ✓ 1/2 teaspoon cayenne
- ✓ 5 tablespoons salted butter
- ✓ 2 large eggs
- ✓ 1/4 teaspoon lemon juice

Preheat oven 350 F.

Combine flour, meal, soda, powder, salt, and cayenne in medium bowl. Cut in butter until crumbly. Add eggs and lemon juice. Stir just until batter comes together.

Spoon batter onto a baking sheet lined with parchment paper in 6 equal domed muffins.

Bake 20 minutes or until tops begin to brown. Cool at least 5 minutes before slicing in half.

Cajun Eggs Benedict

Servings: 6; Net Carbs: 7 g per serving; Calories: 834; Fat: 72 g; Protein: 38 g

- ✓ 1/2 cup unsalted butter
- ✓ 6 ounces boneless, skinless chicken thighs, chopped in 1/2" cubes
- ✓ 1/2 teaspoon Kosher salt
- ✓ 1/4 teaspoon pepper
- ✓ 1/4 pound andouille sausage links, chopped in 1/4" slices
- ✓ 1 teaspoon xanthan gum
- ✓ 1 small green pepper, chopped
- ✓ 1 medium stalk of celery, chopped
- ✓ 1 tablespoon gumbo filé
- ✓ 1 teaspoon cayenne
- ✓ 1-1/2 teaspoon Tabasco
- ✓ 2 tablespoons Worcestershire sauce
- ✓ 4 cloves garlic, minced
- ✓ 1 onion powder
- ✓ 4 cups chicken stock
- ✓ 6 boudin sausage patties
- ✓ 6 eggs
- ✓ 6 Cajun English Muffins (recipe in this book)
- ✓ 6 (2/3 ounce) slices of American cheese

If you are short on time in the morning, you can prepare the gumbo the night before, put it in the refrigerator, and then reheat it before placing it on the muffins.

Heat 2 tablespoons butter in stock pot over medium-high heat. Add chicken, seasoning with salt and pepper, and cook until lightly browned. Remove chicken and add andouille sausage, again cooking until browned and then removing from the pot.

Reduce the heat to medium-low. Add the rest of the butter and the xanthan gum, stirring constantly until the roux thickens and turns brown 5-10 minutes. Then add the pepper, celery, filé, cayenne, Tabasco, Worcestershire, garlic, and onion powder. Cook about 4 minutes, again stirring constantly. Add the stock and the chicken and andouille. Reduce heat to low, cover, and cook for about 1-1/2 hours. Add more salt and pepper to taste, if needed.

Cook boudin sausage patties over medium-high heat in a large skillet, flipping once. Poach eggs. Slice English muffins and place on a microwave safe plate. Place 1/2 slice of cheese on each muffin half. Melt cheese in microwave approximately 15 seconds. Top cheese with one cooked boudin patty, one poached egg, and 1/6 of the gumbo. Finish the sandwich by topping with the other half of the muffin.

.

Cajun Keto Grits

Servings: 1; Net Carbs: 6 g per serving; Calories: 555; Fat: 48 g; Protein: 17 g

- ✓ 1 large egg
- ✓ 1 tablespoon heavy cream
- ✓ 2 teaspoons butter
- ✓ 1 tablespoon diced green pepper
- ✓ 3/4 cup water
- ✓ 2 tablespoons organic ground flax seed
- ✓ 2 tablespoons coconut flour
- ✓ 1/4 cup roasted pecans, coarsely ground
- ✓ 1/4 teaspoon Cajun seasoning
- ✓ 1/8 teaspoon Kosher salt
- ✓ 1 tablespoon crumbled bacon
- ✓ 1 tablespoon grated cheese

Whisk eggs and cream in medium bowl and set aside.

In a medium saucepan, melt the butter and add the diced green pepper, cooking over medium-high heat until tender. Add water, flax seeds, flour, pecans, Cajun seasoning, and salt. Cook until the Keto grits thicken slightly, being sure to stir the mixture frequently.

As soon as the grits are done, remove them from heat and vigorously whisk in the heavy cream mixture until the grits thicken some more and the mixture is well-combined. Serve grits in a bowl with bacon and cheese on top.

Cajun Biscuits and Gravy

Biscuits—Servings: 6; Net Carbs: 5 g per 2 biscuit serving; Calories: 277; Fat: 23 g; Protein: 10 g

Gravy—Servings: 6; Net Carbs: 2 g per serving; Calories: 271; Fat: 21 g; Protein: 17 g

Meal—Servings: 6; Net Carbs: 7 g per serving; Calories: 545; Fat: 44 g; Protein: 27 g

BISCUITS

- ✓ 2 large eggs
- ✓ 1/2 cup sour cream
- ✓ 1/2 teaspoon sea salt
- ✓ 2 cups almond flour
- ✓ 4 teaspoons baking powder

GRAVY

- ✓ 1 tablespoon butter
- ✓ 1 pound pork sausage
- ✓ 1 chicken gizzard, chopped
- ✓ 1 small stalk celery, minced
- ✓ 2 cloves garlic, minced
- ✓ 2 tablespoons red bell pepper, minced
- ✓ 1/2 teaspoon xanthan gum
- ✓ 1/8 teaspoon Worcestershire sauce
- ✓ 1/4 teaspoon Tabasco sauce
- ✓ 2 teaspoon onion powder
- ✓ 1 teaspoon Cajun seasoning
- ✓ 1/4 teaspoon black pepper
- ✓ 1/4 teaspoon Kosher salt
- ✓ 1/4 teaspoon cayenne
- ✓ 2 cups chicken broth

Preheat oven 350 F.

Combine egg, sour cream, and salt in medium bowl. Stir flour and baking powder together in a separate bowl, then fold into the egg mixture using a rubber spatula.

Prepare a baking sheet with parchment. Use 2-tablespoon scoop to scoop the dough into biscuit mounds evenly spaced on the parchment. Do not attempt to flatten the scooped dough.

Bake 15-18 minutes or until tops are golden.

Meanwhile, in a large skillet, melt butter over medium heat. Add pork sausage, gizzard, celery, garlic, and bell peppers. Cook until pork is cooked through. Remove meat and vegetables with a slotted spoon and set aside in a medium bowl.

Turn heat down to medium-low. Add the xanthan gum to the grease mixture remaining in the pan, stirring constantly. Cook until roux is amber in color, about 5-10 minutes, being careful not to burn it.

Add the Worcestershire sauce, Tabasco, onion powder, Cajun seasoning, pepper, salt and cayenne to the roux. Once well combined, add the cooked meats and vegetables back into the roux. Finally, slowly add the stock to the roux, putting in only 1/4 cup at a time and mixing until well-integrated. You may not need all the chicken broth—only add enough to make the gravy the desired thickness.

Cut two biscuits in half and pour 1/6 of the gravy over the top.

Gravy can be frozen in individual serving sizes and reheated as needed.

Cajun Chicken and Waffles

Chicken—Servings: 6; Net Carbs: 2 g per serving; Calories: 238; Fat: 21 g; Protein: 7 g

Gravy—Servings: 6; Net Carbs: 2 g per serving; Calories: 238; Fat: 21 g; Protein: 7 g

Meal—Servings: 8; Net Carbs: 4 g per serving (1/2 waffle and 1 chicken thigh); Calories: 631; Fat: 53 g; Protein: 29 g

CAJUN FRIED CHICKEN
- ✓ 1 large egg
- ✓ 1/4 cup heavy cream
- ✓ 1-1/2 cups crushed pork rinds
- ✓ 1 teaspoon Kosher salt
- ✓ 1/4 teaspoon garlic powder
- ✓ 1/4 teaspoon onion powder
- ✓ 1 tablespoon Cajun seasoning
- ✓ 1/2 teaspoon cayenne (optional)
- ✓ 1/4 cup peanut oil
- ✓ 1 pound boneless, skinless chicken thighs cut into 8 equal pieces

WAFFLES
- ✓ 2-1/2 cups finely ground pecan flour
- ✓ 1 teaspoon xanthan gum
- ✓ 4 teaspoons baking powder
- ✓ 1/4 teaspoon Kosher salt
- ✓ 2 large eggs
- ✓ 1-1/2 cup heavy cream
- ✓ 1 teaspoon vanilla extract
- ✓ 4 tablespoons xylitol or equivalent measurement of the zero carb sweetener of your choice
- ✓ Non-stock cooking spray

Combine egg and heavy cream in medium bowl. In a separate bowl combine crushed pork rinds, salt, garlic, onion, Cajun seasoning, and cayenne if desired.

Heat cooking oil on high. Dip each thigh into the egg and cream mixture first and then dip it in the pork rind mixture. Once the oil is hot, place the thighs into the pan and fry until done, approximately 5 minutes, turning at least once during cooking to ensure they brown evenly. Remove thighs from oil and place on a towel to remove excess oil.

Turn on the waffle iron so it can preheat.

In a large bowl, combine flour, xanthan gum, baking powder, and salt. In a medium bowl, combine eggs, cream, vanilla, and sweetener. Pour the wet ingredients into the dry ingredients, and whisk together.

Spray non-stick cooking spray on the waffle iron. Check the capacity of your waffle iron, but in general, 1 cup of batter should fill it. The carbs are based on half a waffle made with 1 cup of batter.

Follow the manufacturer's instructions for the length of time to cook the waffle, and then unplug the machine or immediately turn it off and allow it to cool 4 minutes before opening it. Use a spatula to help release the waffle from the iron and remove the waffle. Immediately begin reheating the waffle iron for the next waffle. As soon as the waffle iron is hot, spray more non-stick spray and follow the directions again to make the next waffle. Continue until all the waffles are made.

Serve one thigh portion on top of half a waffle.

Pain Perdu

Servings: 1; Net Carbs: 7 g; Calories: 555; Fat: 46 g; Protein: 16 g

- ✓ 2 tablespoons unsalted butter, melted
- ✓ 1 tablespoon xylitol or equivalent measurement of the zero carb sweetener of your choice
- ✓ 1/4 teaspoon vanilla extract
- ✓ 3 tablespoons unsweetened coconut milk
- ✓ 2 tablespoons coconut flour
- ✓ 2 large eggs
- ✓ 1/4 teaspoon cinnamon
- ✓ 1/2 teaspoon baking powder
- ✓ 1 teaspoon unsalted butter
- ✓ 2 medium sliced strawberries
- ✓ 1 tablespoon heavy cream, whipped

Combine 2 tablespoons melted butter, sweetener, vanilla, 2 tablespoons coconut milk, coconut flour, 1 egg, cinnamon, and baking powder in a bowl and whisk until well-combined. Use a rubber spatula to spread the bread "dough" evenly in a 6" glass casserole pan. Bake uncovered in the microwave for 90 seconds or until done. Cool "bread" upside-down over a cutting board for about 5 minutes.

In a medium bowl, whisk together remaining egg and coconut milk.

In a small skillet, heat remaining 1 teaspoon butter over medium-low heat until melted. Dip Keto "bread" in egg mixture, coating both sides. Cook in the butter approximately 3-5 minutes on each side until golden brown, pressing each side gently as it cooks. Top with sliced strawberries and whipped cream.

Cajun Scrambled Egg Rings

Servings: 2; Net Carbs: 4 g; Calories: 381; Fat: 28 g; Protein: 28 g

- ✓ 6 ounces andouille sausage (2 links)
- ✓ 1/2 teaspoon celery salt
- ✓ 1/4 teaspoon garlic powder
- ✓ 1/4 teaspoon onion powder
- ✓ 1/2 teaspoon Cajun seasoning
- ✓ 1 tablespoon butter
- ✓ 4 slices red pepper (to make 1/2" thick rings)
- ✓ 4 large eggs

Cook the sausage in 1/4" of water by bringing the liquid to a boil and cooking 10-15 minutes or follow the package directions.

Combine seasonings in a small bowl and set aside.

Melt butter in a large pan on medium heat. Add bell pepper rings and allow to cook 1-2 minutes. Press the peppers against the pan, and then carefully crack an egg into the center of each ring. Sprinkle each egg with two pinches of the seasoning mix or to taste.

Cook the eggs to your preferred doneness. Flip once if you like over-easy eggs instead of sunny-side-up.

3 LUNCHES

Meaty Red Beans and Cauli Rice

Servings: 8; Net Carbs: 9 g; Calories: 261; Fat: 16 g; Protein: 19 g

- ✓ 1/2 pound dry red beans, soaked
- ✓ 1 ham bone
- ✓ 4 tablespoons butter
- ✓ 1 teaspoon onion powder
- ✓ 1/2 pound andouille sausage, chopped
- ✓ 1/2 pound ham, chopped
- ✓ 1/2 teaspoon thyme
- ✓ 1/2 teaspoon cayenne
- ✓ 1/4 teaspoon black pepper
- ✓ 1/2 teaspoon sage
- ✓ 1 tablespoon parsley
- ✓ 1 tablespoon Cajun seasoning
- ✓ 1 medium stalk celery, chopped
- ✓ 2 cloves garlic, minced
- ✓ 1 small green pepper, chopped
- ✓ 2 tablespoons Worcestershire sauce
- ✓ 1 teaspoon Tabasco sauce
- ✓ 4 cups chicken stock
- ✓ 2-4 cups water
- ✓ 2 bay leaves
- ✓ 4 cups Farm Day Organic cauliflower rice

Prepare the night before in crock-pot.

Sort, rinse, and then prepare beans by boiling in a large pot of water for 10 minutes. Place ham bone in crock-pot.

In a large skillet with butter, combine onion powder, andouille sausage, ham, thyme, cayenne, pepper, sage, parsley, and Cajun seasoning. Cook over medium heat until lightly browned. Use a slotted spoon to scoop out the meat and transfer to the crock pot. Add celery, garlic, and green pepper to the skillet and fry approximately 3-4 minutes or until tender. Add in beans and combine well. Pour beans and vegetables into crock pot. Add Worcestershire sauce, Tabasco, and chicken stock to crock pot and then add more water if needed to cover meat and beans. Place bay leafs on top and cook on low until lunch the next day.

Just before serving, prepare cauliflower rice according to directions. Place 1/2 cup prepared rice in each serving bowl. Remove bay leaves and ham bone from the crock-pot and then stir. Serve 1/8 of the mixture over the cauliflower rice.

Crawdads and Grits

Crawdads—Servings: 4; Net Carbs: 2 g per serving; Calories: 158; Fat: 7 g; Protein: 20 g

Grits—Servings: 4; Net Carbs: 5 g per serving; Calories: 624; Fat: 57 g; Protein: 14 g

Meal—Servings: 4; Net Carbs: 7 g per serving; Calories: 782; Fat: 64 g; Protein: 34 g

KETO GRITS
- ✓ 4 large eggs, beaten
- ✓ 1/4 cup grated cheese
- ✓ 1/4 cup heavy cream
- ✓ 1/2 cup butter
- ✓ 2-3/4 cups water
- ✓ 1/2 cup organic ground flax seed
- ✓ 1/2 cup coconut flour
- ✓ 3/4 cup roasted pecans, coarsely ground
- ✓ 1 teaspoon Cajun seasoning
- ✓ 1 teaspoon black pepper
- ✓ 1 teaspoon onion powder
- ✓ 1/2 teaspoon Kosher salt

CRAWDADS
- ✓ 1 pound crawdads (crawfish), peeled and rinsed
- ✓ 2 tablespoons butter
- ✓ 3 tablespoons diced green pepper
- ✓ 1 medium celery stalk, diced
- ✓ 2 cloves garlic, minced
- ✓ 2 teaspoons onion powder
- ✓ 1 teaspoon Cajun seasoning
- ✓ 1/2 teaspoon cayenne pepper
- ✓ 1/2 cup beef broth

Combine eggs, cheese, and cream in a medium bowl and set aside.

In a medium saucepan, melt the 1/2 cup butter, and add water, flax seeds, flour, pecans, Cajun seasoning, pepper, onion powder, and salt. Cook until the Keto grits thicken slightly, being sure to stir the mixture frequently.

As soon as the grits are done, remove them from heat and vigorously whisk in the egg mixture until the grits thicken some more and the mixture is well-combined. Divide equally into four bowls.

Rinse the crawdads and pat them dry.

In a medium skillet over medium heat, melt the remaining 2 tablespoons butter. Add the green pepper, celery, garlic, and onion powder. Cook approximately 5 minutes until tender. Add crawdads, Cajun seasoning, and cayenne pepper, cooking for another 5 minutes. Then, add the broth and bring to a boil. Set heat to low and simmer another 5 minutes.

Divide crawdad mixture evenly over the grits and serve.

Cajun Crab Cakes

Servings: 2; Net Carbs: 4 g per two crab cake serving; Calories: 509; Fat: 47 g; Protein: 20 g

- ✓ 1 tablespoon Dijon mustard
- ✓ 1/4 cup mayonnaise
- ✓ 1 teaspoon Cajun seasoning
- ✓ 1 teaspoon garlic powder
- ✓ 1-1/2 tablespoons butter
- ✓ 8 ounces crab meat
- ✓ 1 tablespoon fresh parsley, chopped
- ✓ 1 medium stalk celery, chopped
- ✓ 1 tablespoon almond flour
- ✓ 1 large egg
- ✓ 2 tablespoons mayonnaise
- ✓ 1 teaspoon Worcestershire
- ✓ 1/8 teaspoon salt
- ✓ 2 teaspoons Cajun seasoning
- ✓ 1 teaspoon dry mustard, ground
- ✓ 1/2 teaspoon garlic powder
- ✓ 1 teaspoon Tabasco
- ✓ 2 teaspoons lemon juice
- ✓ 1/4 teaspoon cayenne pepper
- ✓ 1/4 teaspoon black pepper

Combine Dijon mustard, mayonnaise, Cajun seasoning, and garlic powder in a small bowl and set aside.

Melt butter in a large skillet over medium heat.

Make sure crabmeat is in fine flakes and parsley and celery have been chopped finely. Combine these and all remaining ingredients in a medium bowl to make the crab cake batter.

Form 4 crab cakes and drop into skillet. Press gently with a spatula to further combine them. Cook about 4-6 minutes until light brown and then carefully flip each cake for an addition 4-6 minutes.

Top with Dijon sauce equally divided between the cakes.

Creole Shrimp Remoulade

Servings: 1; Net Carbs: 6 g; Calories: 625; Fat: 60 g; Protein: 14 g

- ✓ 1/4 cup mayonnaise
- ✓ 1 tablespoon finely chopped green onions
- ✓ 1 tablespoon sugar free ketchup
- ✓ 1 teaspoon fresh parsley, finely chopped
- ✓ 1 teaspoon lemon juice
- ✓ 1 teaspoon capers
- ✓ 1-1/2 teaspoons Dijon mustard
- ✓ 1/2 teaspoon prepared horseradish
- ✓ 1/2 teaspoon garlic, minced
- ✓ 1-1/2 tablespoon salted butter, melted
- ✓ 3/4 teaspoon garlic, minced
- ✓ 1-1/2 teaspoon Cajun seasoning
- ✓ 3/4 teaspoon lemon juice
- ✓ 1/2 teaspoon Worcestershire sauce
- ✓ 1/2 teaspoon celery flakes
- ✓ 1/2 teaspoon onion powder
- ✓ 1/2 teaspoon cayenne
- ✓ 3 ounces uncooked shrimp (about 12 large), peeled and deveined

Turn on oven broiler to preheat or preheat grill.

Combine mayonnaise, green onions, ketchup, parsley, 1 teaspoon lemon juice, capers, Dijon mustard, horseradish, and 1/2 teaspoon garlic to make remoulade in a small bowl. Chill in refrigerator.

Combine butter, remaining garlic, Cajun seasoning, remaining lemon juice, Worcestershire sauce, celery flakes, onion powder, and cayenne in a small bowl.

Skewer shrimp, keeping a little space between each. Brush with butter sauce. If desired, place in refrigerator for up to an hour to marinate.

Broil for about 2 minutes or until shrimp is pink and done. Do not undercook (or overcook) shrimp. You do not need to flip the shrimp during cooking. Alternately, you could grill the shrimp for 5-7 minutes, but you should flip them halfway through cooking if you choose that method.

Serve shrimp with remoulade for dipping.

Shrimp Po'Boys

Bread—Servings: 2; Net Carbs: 8 g; Calories: 808; Fat: 72 g; Protein: 36 g

Filling—Servings: 2; Net Carbs: 4 g*; Calories: 1035*; Fat: 102 g*; Protein: 20 g*

Meal—Servings: 2; Net Carbs: 12 g*; Calories: 1843*; Fat: 174 g*; Protein: 56 g*

BREAD
- ✓ 1 cup almond flour
- ✓ 1 teaspoon double-acting baking powder
- ✓ 1/8 teaspoon Kosher salt
- ✓ 1/4 teaspoon xanthan gum
- ✓ 1/2 cup butter
- ✓ 2 tablespoons coconut oil
- ✓ 6 eggs, separated

FILLING AND SAUCE
- ✓ 1/3 cup mayonnaise
- ✓ 1-1/4 tablespoons Dijon mustard
- ✓ 1/4 teaspoon Tabasco
- ✓ 2 tablespoons canola oil
- ✓ 1 cup pork rinds, crushed
- ✓ 1/4 teaspoon cayenne
- ✓ 1/4 teaspoon salt
- ✓ 1/8 teaspoon black pepper
- ✓ 1 egg, beaten
- ✓ 1/4 cup heavy cream
- ✓ 1/3 cup almond flour
- ✓ 10 ounces large shrimp, shelled and deveined
- ✓ 1 tablespoon salted butter, melted
- ✓ 1 cup shredded lettuce
- ✓ 8 thin (1/8") slices of tomato

Preheat oven 375 F.

In a food processor, combine the dry parts of the bread recipe: flour, baking powder, salt, and xanthan gum as well as the fats: butter and coconut oil. When a dough forms, add in the egg yolks. Blend the egg whites until they reach a soft peak stage. Carefully fold these into the batter and then pour into a parchment lined loaf pan that is greased on the sides with butter. Bake 25- 30 minutes and allow to cool completely.

Combine mayonnaise, Dijon, and Tabasco in a small bowl and set aside.

Heat the oil in a small skillet on medium heat. Combine pork rinds, cayenne, salt, and pepper in one medium bowl. Mix together the egg and cream in another medium bowl. Place the almond flour in a third bowl. Dip each shrimp into the flour, egg, and pork rinds in that order. Then place the shrimp in the pan and fry on both sides until golden and done, approximately 2-3 minutes. Do not over- or under- cook. Transfer the shrimp to a plate covered in paper towels and allow to drain.

Slice the cooled bread in half length-wise and then slice each half in half again parallel to the counter. Place cut-side up on a baking sheet and brush the melted butter over each piece. Cook in the oven at 350 F until toasty. This should take approximately 5 minutes.

Place shrimp, lettuce, and tomato evenly across two pieces of bread. Top with sauce and the remaining two pieces of bread to make two 4" sandwiches.

*Carbs, calories, protein, and fats are a maximum estimate since all the frying oil and breading mixture will not be consumed.

Cajun Shrimp Linguini

Servings: 4; Net Carbs: 7 g; Calories: 381; Fat: 26 g; Protein: 28 g

- ✓ 6 ounces Tofu and Shirataki noodles
- ✓ 1 pound large shrimp, peeled and deveined
- ✓ 1-1/2 teaspoons Cajun seasoning
- ✓ 2 tablespoons canola oil
- ✓ 3 tablespoons diced green pepper
- ✓ 1 medium stalk of celery, thinly sliced
- ✓ 2 teaspoon onion powder
- ✓ 1 teaspoon thyme
- ✓ 1-1/2 teaspoon cayenne pepper
- ✓ 2 cloves garlic, minced
- ✓ 1-14.5 ounce can diced tomatoes, unsalted, undrained
- ✓ 1/3 cup water
- ✓ 3/4 teaspoon Kosher salt
- ✓ 2 bay leaves
- ✓ 1/2 cup heavy cream
- ✓ 1 tablespoon parsley, finely chopped

Fill a medium pot and place on high heat to boil. Rinse noodles under cold water for 2 minutes. Once the water is boiling, place noodles in water for 3 minutes. Drain and rinse under cold water again.

Heat a large non-stick skillet on medium-high heat. Place noodles in skillet and stir to remove excess water. After a few minutes, as soon as noodles are a more dry, remove noodles from pan and place noodles back in strainer to set aside.

Toss shrimp and Cajun seasoning together in a medium bowl. Return skillet to heat and add 1 tablespoon canola oil. Transfer coated shrimp to pan and cook approximately 2-3 minutes until the shrimp are cooked through. Remove shrimp from pan and place in strainer with noodles.

Add the rest of the canola oil to the pan with bell pepper, celery, onion powder and thyme. Cook 5 minutes and add 1/2 teaspoon cayenne and garlic. Cook another 3 minutes and add tomatoes and their juices, 1/3 cup water, salt, and bay leaf. Bring mixture to a boil and reduce heat to low, allowing to thicken for at least 5 minutes while simmering. Remove the bay leaves and discard. Stir in heavy cream. Add shrimp and noodles into sauce, stirring until well combined. Return heat to medium-high, and cook 1 minute until heated through. Divide into four equal portions and sprinkle with 1 teaspoon cayenne and 1 tablespoon parsley.

Cajun Keto Mac and Cheese

Servings: 8; Net Carbs: 7 g; Calories: 330; Fat: 26 g; Protein: 18 g

- ✓ 14 ounces andouille sausage
- ✓ 3 tablespoons diced green pepper
- ✓ 3 tablespoons diced red pepper
- ✓ 1 large head of cauliflower
- ✓ 1/4 teaspoon salt
- ✓ 1/4 teaspoon black pepper
- ✓ 1 cup heavy cream
- ✓ 2 teaspoons Cajun seasoning
- ✓ 1 teaspoon onion powder
- ✓ 1 teaspoon garlic powder
- ✓ 3 ounces cream cheese
- ✓ 1 cup cheddar cheese
- ✓ 1/2 cup mozzarella cheese
- ✓ 1/4 cup parmesan cheese
- ✓ Non-stick cooking spray

Preheat oven 375 F.

Cook the sausage over medium heat in a large skillet until browned. Add green and red bell peppers. Continue cooking until peppers are tender. Remove from heat and set aside.

Cut cauliflower into florets and steam in the microwave with a tablespoon of water. Strain the water and toss cauliflower with sausage, peppers, salt and pepper. Place mixture in a baking dish that has been prepared with non-stick cooking spray.

In a medium saucepan, heat cream, Cajun seasoning, onion powder, and garlic powder. Add cream cheese, cheddar, and mozzarella, stirring after each addition until sauce is smooth. Pour cheese sauce over cauliflower and top with parmesan. Bake 15-20 minutes until top has browned slightly.

4 DINNERS

Keto Jambalaya

Servings: 6; Net Carbs: 6 g; Calories: 354; Fat: 17 g; Protein: 41 g

- ✓ 2 tablespoons salted butter
- ✓ 3/4 pound andouille sausage
- ✓ 1 pound boneless, skinless chicken thighs, cut into 1" cubes
- ✓ 1 tablespoon onion powder
- ✓ 2 medium stalk of celery, chopped
- ✓ 4 small green pepper, chopped
- ✓ 1 cloves garlic, minced
- ✓ 2-1/2 cups chicken stock
- ✓ 1-1/2 cups canned diced tomatoes and green chilies, drained
- ✓ 1 teaspoon thyme
- ✓ 1 teaspoon Kosher salt
- ✓ 1/2 teaspoon black pepper
- ✓ 1/2 teaspoon smoked paprika
- ✓ 1/4 teaspoon cayenne
- ✓ 1 tablespoon parsley, chopped finely
- ✓ 3 cups cauliflower rice
- ✓ 12 ounces shrimp, peeled and deveined

Melt butter in a Dutch oven over medium-high heat. Add sausage and chicken, cooking until browned approximately 5 minutes. Add onion, celery, bell pepper, and garlic, cooking until tender approximately 3 more minutes. Add stock, tomatoes, thyme, salt, pepper, paprika, cayenne, and parsley. Bring to a boil and reduce heat to medium-low.

Add cauliflower rice and cook 7 minutes. Add shrimp, and cook until they are done, approximately 2-3 minutes. Divide into 6 even portions.

Blackened Salmon and Dirty Cauli Rice

Salmon—Servings: 4; Net Carbs: 2 g; Calories: 356; Fat: 26 g; Protein: 26 g

Rice—Servings: 4; Net Carbs: 2 g; Calories: 222; Fat: 13 g; Protein: 24 g

Meal—Servings: 4; Net Carbs: 4 g; Calories: 578; Fat: 39 g; Protein: 50 g

SALMON
- ✓ 2 tablespoons paprika
- ✓ 1 tablespoon onion powder
- ✓ 1/4 teaspoon thyme
- ✓ 1/2 teaspoon black pepper
- ✓ 1 tablespoon cayenne
- ✓ 2 teaspoons salt
- ✓ 1/4 teaspoon basil
- ✓ 1/4 teaspoon oregano
- ✓ 4 tablespoons butter, melted
- ✓ 16 ounces salmon divided into 4-4 ounce filets

RICE
- ✓ 1 tablespoon bacon grease
- ✓ 8 ounces ground beef
- ✓ 1/3 cup celery, chopped
- ✓ 1/3 cup green pepper, chopped
- ✓ 1 teaspoon onion powder
- ✓ 2 cloves garlic, minced
- ✓ 4 ounces chicken livers, finely chopped
- ✓ 1-1/4 cup chicken stock
- ✓ 1 bay leaf
- ✓ 1/4 teaspoon thyme
- ✓ 2 teaspoons paprika
- ✓ 1/4 teaspoon cayenne
- ✓ 1/4 teaspoon Kosher salt

- ✓ 1/8 teaspoon Tabasco
- ✓ 2 teaspoon Cajun seasoning
- ✓ 2-2/3 cups cauliflower rice
- ✓ 2 small green onions, thinly sliced

Combine salmon blackening spices in medium bowl.

Place medium skillet on high heat. Brush butter on both sides of salmon and press into blackening spices. Dump any remaining butter into the skillet. Cook salmon in butter until blackened, approximately 3-5 minutes. Flip filets and cook the other side until fish flakes with a fork.

In a Dutch oven, heat bacon grease, ground beef, celery, green pepper, and onion powder. Cook until vegetables are tender and beef is browned approximately 6 minutes. Add garlic and chicken livers, cooking an additional 5 minutes.

Pour broth into pot scraping the bottom to release pieces that are stuck. Add bay leaf, thyme, paprika, cayenne, salt, Tabasco, Cajun seasoning, and cauliflower rice. Simmer approximately 10 minutes until rice is cooked and most of the liquid has evaporated. Remove from heat. Remove the bay leaf and discard.

Place one filet of salmon on each plate and evenly divide the rice between the four servings. Garnish with green onions.

Keto Gumbo

Servings: 6; Net Carbs: 5 g; Calories: 407; Fat: 21 g; Protein: 45 g

- ✓ 1/4 cup unsalted butter
- ✓ 1 pound boneless skinless chicken thigh
- ✓ 4 ounces andouille sausage
- ✓ 1 teaspoon xanthan gum
- ✓ 1 cloves garlic, minced
- ✓ 1 small green pepper, chopped
- ✓ 2 teaspoons onion powder
- ✓ 2 medium stalks of celery, chopped
- ✓ 3 cups chicken stock
- ✓ 1/4 pound crab legs
- ✓ 1-1/2 teaspoons Cajun seasoning
- ✓ 1 cube chicken bullion
- ✓ 1/4 teaspoon pepper
- ✓ 3/4 teaspoon smoked paprika
- ✓ 1 bay leaves
- ✓ 1/2 teaspoon thyme
- ✓ 3/4 cups canned diced tomatoes and green chilies, drained
- ✓ 1/2 pound shrimp
- ✓ 3-3/4 cups Farm Day Organic cauliflower rice
- ✓ 1-1/2 teaspoons gumbo filé
- ✓ 1 small green onion, finely sliced
- ✓ 2 tablespoons parsley, finely chopped

In a Dutch oven over medium heat, melt half the butter and add the chicken, browning on both sides. Remove the chicken and set aside. Add the sausage, again cooking until browned and remove.

Add the rest of the butter to the Dutch oven and the xanthan gum, stirring continuously until it turns chocolate brown in color. This can take up to 30 minutes, and you must stir frequently or it will burn. As soon as it turns the right color, remove it from the stove and allow it to cool.

Once you are ready to begin again, place the Dutch oven back on the stove with the garlic, green pepper, onion powder, and celery. Cook the vegetables until they are tender, continuing to frequently stir them. This should take approximately 8 minutes.

Return the chicken and sausage to the pot. Add the chicken stock, crab legs, Cajun seasoning, bullion cube, pepper, paprika, bay leaves, thyme, and tomatoes. Simmer on low for 55 minutes.

Add the shrimp, cauliflower rice, and any remaining ingredients and allow to simmer 5-10 more minutes until the cauliflower rice and shrimp are done. You may add water and/or salt to adjust the flavor and thickness to your desired taste.

Fried Catfish and Keto Hushpuppies

Catfish—Servings: 6; Net Carbs: 2 g*; Calories: 380*; Fat: 31 g*; Protein: 22 g

Hushpuppies—Servings: 6; Net Carbs: 5 g*; Calories: 267*; Fat: 24 g*; Protein: 9 g*

Meal—Servings: 6; Net Carbs: 7 g*; Calories: 647*; Fat: 55 g*; Protein: 31 g*

FRYING OIL
- ✓ 2 cups peanut oil

HUSHPUPPIES
- ✓ 2 large eggs
- ✓ 1/2 cup sour cream
- ✓ 3 drops cornbread extract
- ✓ 1 teaspoon onion powder
- ✓ 1/2 teaspoon sea salt
- ✓ 1-1/2 cups almond meal
- ✓ 3/4 cups crushed pork rinds
- ✓ 4 teaspoons baking powder

CATFISH
- ✓ 18 ounces catfish, filleted in 6 pieces
- ✓ 1 cup heavy cream
- ✓ 1 cup pork rinds, crushed
- ✓ 1/2 teaspoon cayenne
- ✓ 1/2 cup almond flour
- ✓ 1/4 teaspoon salt
- ✓ 1/8 teaspoon black pepper

Heat oil in small skillet over medium heat.

Place catfish in a bowl, pour cream over the top, and allow to soak in the refrigerator.

For the hushpuppies, combine egg, sour cream, cornbread extract, onion powder, and salt in medium bowl. Stir almond meal, pork rinds, and baking powder together in a separate bowl, then fold this mixture into the egg mixture using a rubber spatula. Use 2-tablespoon scoop to scoop the dough into the hot oil. Do not over-fill the skillet. Let hushpuppies become golden brown and then remove from oil and place on paper towel to drain.

Pour most of the oil out of the pan and into a mug to reserve it.

For the salmon breading, combine pork rinds, cayenne, flour, salt, and pepper in one medium bowl. Retrieve the catfish from the refrigerator. Dip each catfish into the pork rind mixture. Then place the catfish in the pan and fry on both sides until golden and done, approximately 2-3 minutes per side. Do not over- or under- cook. You should be able to flake the fish with a fork. Transfer the catfish to the plate covered in paper towels and allow to drain.

*Carbs, calories, protein, and fats are a estimated since all the frying oil cream, and breading mixture will not be consumed.

Alligator* Steak and Keto Fried Green Tomatoes

Sauce—Servings: 4; Net Carbs: 2 g; Calories: 200; Fat: 21 g; Protein: 1 g

Alligator—Servings: 4; Net Carbs: 1 g; Calories: 134; Fat: 5 g; Protein: 20 g

Tomatoes—Servings: 4; Net Carbs: 3 g*; Calories: 135*; Fat: 11 g*; Protein: 5 g*

Meal—Servings: 4; Net Carbs: 6 g*; Calories: 470*; Fat: 37 g*; Protein: 26 g*

SAUCE
- ✓ 1/2 cup mayonnaise
- ✓ 2 tablespoons sugar free ketchup
- ✓ 1 teaspoon cayenne pepper
- ✓ 1 teaspoon Worcestershire sauce
- ✓ 1/4 teaspoon Kosher salt
- ✓ 1/4 teaspoon Tabasco
- ✓ 1/4 teaspoon black pepper
- ✓ 1/4 teaspoon onion powder
- ✓ 1/4 teaspoon garlic powder
- ✓ 1 teaspoon Cajun seasoning
- ✓ 1 tablespoons chili sauce
- ✓ 1 teaspoon lemon juice

ALLIGATOR
- ✓ 1 pound alligator sirloin
- ✓ 2 tablespoons Cajun seasoning
- ✓ 1 teaspoon garlic powder
- ✓ 2 teaspoons olive oil

TOMATOES
- ✓ 1 egg
- ✓ 1/4 cup crushed pork rinds
- ✓ 1/4 cup almond meal
- ✓ 1/4 teaspoon Kosher salt

- ✓ 1/8 teaspoon black pepper
- ✓ 1/8 teaspoon garlic powder
- ✓ 12 medium (1/4") slices green tomatoes
- ✓ 2 tablespoons butter

Combine all the ingredients for the sauce and set aside.

Rinse the alligator and pat it dry. Cut into pieces so it can easily be divided into four equal portions and so each piece can be skewered.

Mix the Cajun seasoning and garlic together. Rub olive oil into the alligator meat and then rub seasoning and garlic mixture into the meat. Allow meat to stand at least 30 minutes at room temperature.

Melt butter in a small skillet on medium heat. Whisk egg lightly in medium bowl. Combine pork rinds, almond meal, salt, pepper, and garlic in another medium bowl. Dip each tomato slice into the egg and then into the pork rind mixture. Cook in butter until golden brown flipping halfway through cooking. Drain on paper towel.

Preheat broiler or grill. Skewer alligator meat. Broil for about 3-5 minutes per side or until done. Do not undercook (or overcook) it. Alternately, you could grill the alligator for 5-7 minutes per side.

*3 ounces chicken can be substituted for alligator.

*Carbs, calories, protein, and fats are a estimated since all the frying oil cream, and breading mixture will not be consumed.

Cajun Fried Chicken and Okra

Chicken—Servings: 4; Net Carbs: 4 g*; Calories: 595*; Fat: 41 g*; Protein: 49 g*

Okra—Servings: 4; Net Carbs: 6 g*; Calories: 221*; Fat: 19 g*; Protein: 7 g*

Meal—Servings: 4; Net Carbs: 10 g*; Calories: 816*; Fat: 60 g*; Protein: 56 g*

CHICKEN
- ✓ 2 eggs
- ✓ 2 teaspoons Dijon mustard
- ✓ 1 teaspoon salt
- ✓ 1 teaspoon black pepper
- ✓ 2 teaspoons Cajun seasoning
- ✓ 1 teaspoon garlic
- ✓ 1/2 teaspoon paprika
- ✓ 1/2 teaspoon cayenne
- ✓ 1 cup finely grated (fresh) cheddar cheese
- ✓ 3/4 cup almond meal
- ✓ 4 tablespoons peanut oil
- ✓ 1-pound boneless, skinless chicken breasts cut into 8 tenders or 8 pre-cut tenders

OKRA
- ✓ 1/2 cup heavy cream
- ✓ 1/4 cup crushed pork rinds
- ✓ 1/2 cup almond flour
- ✓ 1/4 teaspoon Kosher salt
- ✓ 1/8 teaspoon black pepper
- ✓ 1/8 teaspoon garlic powder
- ✓ 1/4 teaspoon Cajun seasoning
- ✓ 3/4 pound fresh okra, sliced thickly

Whisk together eggs, Dijon, salt, pepper, Cajun seasoning, garlic, paprika, and cayenne in a small bowl. Toss together the cheese and almond meal in a separate bowl.

Heat cooking oil on high until hot. Dip each tender first in the egg mixture and then in the cheese mixture. Place them in the oil to cook until done, approximately 5 minutes. Remove from oil and place on a paper towel.

Reduce oil heat to medium.

Pour cream in small bowl. Combine pork rinds, flour, salt, pepper, garlic, and Cajun seasoning in a medium bowl. Dip each okra slice into the cream and then into the pork rind mixture. Cook in oil until golden brown, flipping halfway through cooking. Drain on paper towel.

*Carbs, calories, protein, and fats are a estimated since all the frying oil cream, and breading mixture will not be consumed.

Keto Crawdad Étouffée

Servings: 5; Net Carbs: 5 g per 1 cup étouffée and ½ cup rice; Calories: 203; Fat: 11 g; Protein: 18 g

- ✓ 4 tablespoons salted butter, softened
- ✓ 2 small green pepper, chopped
- ✓ 4 medium stalk of celery, chopped
- ✓ 3 cloves garlic, minced
- ✓ 2 teaspoons onion powder
- ✓ 1 teaspoon xanthan gum
- ✓ 1 teaspoon cayenne
- ✓ 2 teaspoons Cajun seasoning
- ✓ 2- 8 ounce bottles clam juice
- ✓ 1/4 teaspoon thyme
- ✓ 1 cup canned diced tomatoes and green chilies, unsalted, drained
- ✓ 1/4 teaspoon salt
- ✓ 1 teaspoon Worcestershire sauce
- ✓ 1 pound crawdad/crawfish tail meat, cooked and cleaned
- ✓ 2-1/2 cups Farm Day Organic cauliflower rice
- ✓ 1/4 cup thinly sliced green onions

In a Dutch oven, melt 1 tablespoon of the butter and add bell pepper, celery, garlic, and onion powder, cooking 8 minutes or until vegetables are tender.

Remove vegetable mixture using slotted spoon and set aside in bowl. Add remaining butter, xanthan gum, cayenne, and Cajun seasoning, stirring constantly until a rust-colored roux is formed, approximately 6 minutes.

Add clam juice and thyme and continue cooking 1 more minute. Add vegetable mixture, tomatoes, salt, and Worcestershire sauce. Simmer for 15 minutes and add the crawdad tails. Continue cooking until crawdads are heated through, approximately 6 more minutes.

Steam the cauliflower rice in the microwave according to the directions on the package. Place 1/2 cup of rice in a bowl and top with étouffée divided into five equal portions. Use the green onions for garnish.

5 SNACKS

Cajun Deviled Eggs

Servings: 12; Net Carbs: 1 g; Calories: 113; Fat: 9 g; Protein: 7 g

- ✓ 2 tablespoons vinegar (optional)
- ✓ pinch of salt (optional)
- ✓ 12 eggs
- ✓ 1 medium avocado, ripe
- ✓ 2 tablespoons mayonnaise
- ✓ 1 tablespoon Cajun seasoning
- ✓ 1/4 teaspoon black pepper
- ✓ 1/8 teaspoon salt
- ✓ 1 teaspoon celery flakes
- ✓ 1 teaspoon cayenne
- ✓ 1 tablespoon bell pepper, finely diced

Adding 2 teaspoons white vinegar and a pinch of salt to the boiling water while you are making the eggs may help the shells come off. As soon as the eggs come to a boil, boil them over the heat for 2 minutes, cover them, and remove them from the heat for another 11 minutes. Then soak them in freezing ice water for 3 minutes before peeling.

Once peeled, cut the eggs in half placing the yolks in a large bowl and the white halves on a tray. Stir avocado, mayonnaise, Cajun seasoning, pepper, salt, and celery flakes into the yolks.

Fill a piping bag with mayonnaise mixture and pipe it into each egg-white half. Sprinkle with cayenne and bell pepper.

Cajun Biscuit Bombs

Servings: 12; Net Carbs: 3 g per serving; Calories: 322; Fat: 29 g; Protein: 11 g

BISCUITS

- ✓ 1/2 pound pork sausage
- ✓ 2 cups almond flour
- ✓ 1/2 teaspoon sea salt
- ✓ 4 teaspoons baking powder
- ✓ 1 teaspoon cayenne pepper
- ✓ 1 teaspoon onion powder
- ✓ 1/4 cup bacon fat
- ✓ 3/4 cup cheddar cheese, shredded
- ✓ 2 ounces diced green chilies
- ✓ 3/4 cup heavy cream
- ✓ Non-stick cooking spray

Preheat oven 400 F.

Cook sausage in a medium skillet over medium heat until browned and fully cooked. Place in refrigerator to cool.

Spray muffin pan with non-stick cooking spray.

Combine flour, salt, baking powder cayenne, and onion powder together in a separate bowl, then cut in bacon fat. Add cooked sausage, chilies, and cheese to flour mixture. Slowly stir in cream. The mixture should be very wet, but hold together.

Evenly distribute batter between muffin cups, rounding the tops. Bake 15-20 minutes or until tops are golden brown.

Creole Cauliflower-Onion Bloom

Servings: 8; Net Carbs: 8 g; Calories: 641*; Fat: 60 g*; Protein: 17 g*

- ✓ 1-1/2 cups heavy cream
- ✓ 1 teaspoon celery salt
- ✓ 1 teaspoon pepper
- ✓ 1 tablespoon onion powder
- ✓ 2 tablespoons Tabasco
- ✓ 1 large head cauliflower
- ✓ 1-1/2 cups butter
- ✓ 1 teaspoon oregano
- ✓ 1 teaspoon ground cumin
- ✓ 2 teaspoons garlic powder
- ✓ 1 teaspoon salt
- ✓ 1 teaspoon paprika
- ✓ 2 teaspoons cayenne
- ✓ 1-1/2 cups almond flour
- ✓ 1-1/2 cups parmesan cheese
- ✓ 4 eggs

Mix cream, celery salt, pepper, onion powder, and Tabasco in a medium bowl. Cut cauliflower into 8 equal pieces and place in bowl. Pour cream mixture over cauliflower and place in refrigerator to marinate for 30-60 minutes.

Preheat the butter in a large skillet over medium heat.

In a large, zip-close, freezer bag, combine oregano, cumin, garlic, salt, paprika, cayenne, almond flour, and parmesan cheese.

As soon as you get the cauliflower out of the cream mixture, allow the excess to drip off. Reserve the cream mixture. Place the cauliflower in the flour mixture, seal the bag and gently shake to coat. Remove cauliflower, shaking gently to remove excess breading.

Beat the eggs into the cream mixture. Dip the coated cauliflower pieces in the egg mixture, again allowing excess to drip off, and then transfer back to the flour mixture, again shaking to coat a second time.

Lower the breaded cauliflower into the butter carefully. Fry until golden brown on all sides. Use a slotted spoon to lift the cauliflower out of the butter and place it on a plate with paper towel to drain.

*Calories, protein, and fats are estimated since all the cream and breading mixtures will not be used.

Cajun Nut Mix

Servings: 20; Net Carbs: 4 g per half cup serving; Calories: 417; Fat: 42 g; Protein: 8 g

- ✓ 4 teaspoons xylitol or equivalent measurement of the zero carb sweetener of your choice
- ✓ 1-1/2 tablespoon seasoned salt
- ✓ 1 teaspoon onion powder
- ✓ 1 teaspoon paprika
- ✓ 1/2 teaspoon cayenne pepper
- ✓ 1/2 teaspoon garlic powder
- ✓ 2-1/4 teaspoon black pepper
- ✓ 1/8 teaspoon dry mustard, ground
- ✓ 1/8 teaspoon oregano
- ✓ 1/8 teaspoon thyme
- ✓ 4 tablespoons bacon grease
- ✓ 4 cups unsalted pecans
- ✓ 2 cups unsalted hazelnuts
- ✓ 2 cups unsalted almonds
- ✓ 2 cups unsalted macadamia nuts

Preheat oven 200 F.

Combine sweetener with all the seasonings, salt, and spices in a small bowl. Combine nuts in a separate, large bowl, tossing to mix well. Melt bacon grease and drizzle over nuts, tossing again to mix well. Sprinkle seasoning mix over the top of the nuts and toss again.

Place a piece of parchment paper on a large baking sheet and spread nut mixture evenly across the top of it. Place in oven and bake 45 minutes, stirring every 15 minutes. Store in an airtight container.

Avocado Shrimp Cocktail

Servings: 4; Net Carbs: 4 g; Calories: 296; Fat: 20 g; Protein: 24 g

- ✓ 2 avocados
- ✓ 1 tablespoon lemon juice
- ✓ 3 tablespoons mayonnaise
- ✓ 1 tablespoon heavy cream
- ✓ 1/8 teaspoon Tabasco
- ✓ 2 tablespoons Worcestershire sauce
- ✓ 1/8 teaspoon salt
- ✓ 1/8 teaspoon black pepper
- ✓ 1-1/2 cups baby shrimp, cooked and peeled
- ✓ 1/2 teaspoon cayenne

Cut avocados in half and remove pit. Sprinkle lemon juice on exposed flesh.

In a medium bowl, cream together mayonnaise, cream, Tabasco, Worcestershire sauce, salt, and pepper. Fold shrimp into the mayonnaise mixture. Spoon into hole left by the pit in the avocado halves. Sprinkle with cayenne.

Chill until just before serving.

Boudin Balls

Servings: 8; Net Carbs: 2 g; Calories: 383*; Fat: 36 g*; Protein: 12 g

- ✓ 1 cup bacon grease
- ✓ 1 pound boudin sausage
- ✓ 2 large eggs
- ✓ 1-1/2 cups crushed pork rinds
- ✓ 1/8 teaspoon salt
- ✓ 1 teaspoon Cajun seasoning

Heat bacon grease over medium heat in a large skillet.

Remove casing from boudin. Form sausage into 1" balls.

In a small bowl, beat eggs slightly. Combine pork rinds, salt, and Cajun seasoning. Dip boudin into beaten egg and then dip into pork rind mixture, coating well.

Deep fry coated boudin until lightly browned and allow it to drain on a paper towel before serving.

*Calories and fats are estimated since all the bacon grease will not be used.

Cajun Crab Puffs

Servings: 12; Net Carbs: 2 g; Calories: 276; Fat: 25 g; Protein: 11 g

- ✓ 1/2 cup flaked crabmeat
- ✓ 1/2 cup crawdads/crawfish, cleaned, cooked, and chopped
- ✓ 1 teaspoon onion powder
- ✓ 1 medium green onion, sliced thinly
- ✓ 1 small green pepper, diced
- ✓ 1 teaspoon mustard powder
- ✓ 1 teaspoon Worcestershire sauce
- ✓ 2 teaspoons Tabasco
- ✓ 1 cup cheddar cheese, grated
- ✓ 1-1/2 cups water
- ✓ 3/4 cup butter
- ✓ 1/2 teaspoon salt
- ✓ 1-1/2 cups almond flour
- ✓ 6 eggs

Preheat oven 400 F.

Combine crab, crawdads, onion powder, onion, and bell pepper in medium bowl. Stir in mustard, Worcestershire sauce, Tabasco, and cheese.

In a medium saucepan over medium-high heat, bring water, butter, and salt to a boil. Reduce heat to low and add flour while stirring vigorously. Continue stirring until mixture forms a smooth ball. Remove from heat and cool slightly.

Using a wooden spoon beat eggs into flour mixture one at a time, then continue beating until batter is smooth again. Add the crab mixture and stir well.

Drop by rounded teaspoon onto an ungreased baking sheet and bake 15 minutes. Reduce heat to 350 F and continue baking approximately 10 more minutes until golden brown.

Serve hot or store in freezer and reheat by completely thawing and then baking at 350 F for 8-10 minutes.

6 DESSERTS

Bananas Foster Keto Style

Servings: 6; Net Carbs: 1 g; Calories: 234; Fat: 15 g; Protein: 4 g

- ✓ 1/2 cup unsweetened coconut milk
- ✓ 1/4 teaspoon sea salt
- ✓ 1/2 cup xylitol or equivalent measurement of the zero carb sweetener of your choice
- ✓ 1/2 cup unsalted butter
- ✓ 3 drops banana oil (or 1 teaspoon banana extract)
- ✓ 1/2 teaspoon rum extract
- ✓ 3/4 cup heavy cream
- ✓ 3 large eggs
- ✓ 1/2 cup xylitol or equivalent measurement of the zero carb sweetener of your choice
- ✓ 3/4 teaspoon vanilla extract
- ✓ 1/4 teaspoon sea salt

Please read through the recipe and make sure you understand it before attempting to do it. Many steps require you to move seamlessly to the next one.

Whisk together coconut milk, salt, and sweetener in a pitcher.

In a small saucepan, melt the butter and cook it on high heat until it boils and specks of brown appear. Immediately pour in coconut milk mixture, slowly and vigorously whisk until sauce is smooth. Remove from heat. Continue whisking as you add in the oil and extract. Place in the refrigerator to cool. You can store syrup covered in the refrigerator up to two weeks.

Begin water boiling in a double boiler.

Whisk heavy cream until it forms stiff peaks and place in the refrigerator.

Whisk together eggs, sweetener, vanilla, and salt in the top of the double boiler when it is off the heat. Once they are well combined, place a thermometer in them and place them over the heat. Turn the stove to high and continue whisking vigorously and scraping the sides continuously. As soon as the thermometer hits 160 F, remove the mixture from the heat and transfer to a stand mixer. Beat on high speed for about 6-8 minutes.

Fold the egg mixture gently into the whipped cream mixture. Spread in an 8 x 8 square pan and freeze, covered, for at least 8 hours. You may have to let it set out for approximately 10 minutes before you cut it into 6 equal squares.

Top the ice cream with 1/6 the cooled banana syrup.

Bread Pudding and Salted Caramel Sauce

Bread Pudding—Servings: 8; Net Carbs: 5 g per slice; Calories: 618; Fat: 60 g; Protein: 13 g

Caramel Sauce—Servings: 8; Net Carbs: 1 g (3 tablespoons sauce); Calories: 289; Fat: 30 g; Protein: 1 g

Dessert Servings: 8; Net Carbs: 6 g (1 slice bread and 3 tablespoons sauce); Calories: 907; Fat: 90 g; Protein: 14 g

BREAD PUDDING

- ✓ 1 cup almond flour
- ✓ 1 teaspoon double-acting baking powder
- ✓ 1/8 teaspoon Kosher salt
- ✓ 1/4 teaspoon xanthan gum
- ✓ 1/2 cup butter
- ✓ 2 tablespoons coconut oil
- ✓ 6 eggs, separated
- ✓ 2 cups chopped pecans
- ✓ 3 cups heavy cream
- ✓ 3 large eggs
- ✓ 8 teaspoons xylitol or equivalent measurement of the zero carb sweetener of your choice
- ✓ 1 teaspoon vanilla extract
- ✓ 2 teaspoons cinnamon
- ✓ 1 teaspoon nutmeg
- ✓ Non-stick cooking spray

SALTED CARAMEL SAUCE

- ✓ 2/3 cup butter
- ✓ 1/4 cup xylitol or equivalent measurement of the zero carb sweetener of your choice
- ✓ 1-1/3 cup heavy cream
- ✓ 2 teaspoons vanilla extract
- ✓ 2 teaspoons maple extract
- ✓ 1 teaspoons sea salt

Preheat oven 375 F.

In a food processor, combine the bread recipe flour, baking powder, salt, and xanthan gum and then pulse in the butter and coconut oil. When a dough forms, add in the egg yolks. Blend the egg whites until they reach a soft peak stage. Carefully fold these into the batter and then pour into a parchment lined sheet pan that is greased on the sides with butter. Bake 25- 30 minutes and allow to cool completely.

In a medium saucepan, melt the butter for the caramel sauce over medium-low heat. Add sweetener and continue to cook for 3-4 minutes, stirring occasionally and watching closely to prevent burning.

Stir in the heavy cream and continue heating until mixture comes to a gentle boil. Reduce heat to low and simmer, stirring occasionally, until the mixture coats the back of the spoon and is a caramel color. This can take up to 45 minutes.

Remove from heat and whisk in extracts and sea salt. (Unused portions of the caramel sauce need to be kept in the refrigerator and can be gently reheated if needed.) Stir before using.

Turn oven to 250 F. Once the bread has cooled, cut it into 1" to 2" cubes. Place on baking sheet in a disorganized manner (i.e. don't just cut the bread and return it to the oven without stirring it up some). Bake another 30 minutes to 1 hour until bread has dried out some, but is not crisp. Alternately, you could leave the bread out overnight instead of baking it again.

Spray a loaf pan with non-stick cooking spray. Toss pecans with the bread cubes and pour into loaf pan.

In a medium bowl, combine cream, egg, sweetener, vanilla, cinnamon, and nutmeg. Pour over the bread mixture, press bread gently into liquid, cover, and refrigerate 1 hour.

Preheat oven to 350 F. Remove cover from bread pudding and bake for approximately 1 hour until the top is golden brown. Allow to cool completely before cutting. Cut into 8 slices. Serve with 3 tablespoons of caramel sauce on top of each slice.

Keto King Cake

Cake—Servings: 8; Net Carbs: 3 g per slice; Calories: 445; Fat: 30 g; Protein: 9 g

Frosting—Servings: 8; Net Carbs: 0 g; Calories: 67*; Fat: 3 g*; Protein: 0 g

Total Servings: 8; Net Carbs: 4 g; Calories: 512*; Fat: 33 g*; Protein: 9 g

CAKE

- ✓ 1/4 teaspoon cream of tartar
- ✓ 5 large eggs, separated
- ✓ 6 tablespoons butter, melted
- ✓ 1-1/2 teaspoons cinnamon
- ✓ 1/4 cup + 1 tablespoon xylitol or equivalent measurement of the zero carb sweetener of your choice
- ✓ 2/3 cup toasted pecans, chopped
- ✓ 1/2 teaspoon bourbon extract
- ✓ 1/2 teaspoon orange zest
- ✓ 1/8 teaspoon ground nutmeg
- ✓ 2 teaspoons baking powder
- ✓ 1 cup almond flour
- ✓ 1 teaspoon vanilla extract
- ✓ 4 ounces cream cheese, softened
- ✓ Non-stick cooking spray

FROSTING

- ✓ 6 teaspoons xylitol or equivalent measurement of the zero carb sweetener of your choice
- ✓ 1/8 teaspoon powdered green food coloring
- ✓ 1/8 teaspoon powdered yellow food coloring
- ✓ 1/8 teaspoon powdered purple food coloring
- ✓ 2 tablespoons butter, softened
- ✓ 1 ounce cream cheese, softened
- ✓ 2-3 tablespoons heavy cream

- ✓ 3 tablespoons xylitol or equivalent measurement of the zero carb sweetener of your choice, ground in a food processor until powdered sugar consistency
- ✓ 1/2 teaspoon vanilla extract

Preheat oven 350 F.

Add cream of tartar to the separated egg whites and beat until they form soft peaks. Set aside.

In a small bowl, combine 3 tablespoons butter, cinnamon, and 1/4 cup of sweetener, pecans, bourbon extract, and orange zest. Set aside.

Sift together nutmeg, baking powder, and flour.

Combine egg yolks, remaining cake butter, vanilla, cream cheese, and remaining 1 tablespoon cake sweetener. Add in flour mixture and mix well. Fold egg whites into batter.

Grease a Bundt pan with non-stick cooking spray being careful to only spray the bottom of the pan and not the sides.

Pour half the flour batter into the Bundt pan. Place the pecan mixture in a piping bag with a wide tip and pipe a ring around the center of the batter. Cover the pecan mixture with the remaining flour batter. (At this point you can press a toy/baby into the batter and hide it if you wish.)

Bake 30-40 minutes or until top is golden brown. Cool completely before removing from pan.

To prepare the icing, first place 2 tablespoons of sweetener in three separate small bowls (using a total of 6 tablespoons). Add a different color of powdered food coloring to each bowl and mix well until the color is uniform. Set the three bowls aside.

In another medium bowl, combine icing cream cheese, butter, vanilla, remaining icing sweetener, and 2 tablespoons of heavy cream, whisking until smooth. Use the additional tablespoon of heavy cream to adjust the thickness of the frosting.

Remove cake from pan. Drizzle frosting over the cake. Sprinkle different colors of the powdered sweetener over the top before the frosting sets.

*Calories and fats are estimated based on all the cream being used, numbers will be slightly lower if all the cream is not used.

Keto Pecan Tart

Servings: 8; Net Carbs: 3 g; Calories: 356; Fat: 33 g; Protein: 6 g

- ✓ 1-1/4 cup almond meal
- ✓ 1/4 cup ground flax seeds
- ✓ 1 teaspoon cinnamon
- ✓ 7 tablespoons xylitol or equivalent measurement of the zero carb sweetener of your choice
- ✓ 2 tablespoons coconut oil
- ✓ 3/4 teaspoon salt
- ✓ 1-3 tablespoons water
- ✓ 6 tablespoons butter
- ✓ 3/4 cup heavy cream
- ✓ 1 teaspoon vanilla extract
- ✓ 1/2 teaspoon maple extract
- ✓ 1 large egg
- ✓ 1 cup pecans, chopped coarsely

Preheat oven 350 F.

In a food processor, pulse together almond meal, flax, cinnamon, 1 tablespoon sweetener, coconut oil, and 1/4 teaspoon salt until mixture combines to a crumb. Slowly add water until a ball forms. Press dough into a 7-1/2" tart pan (dough may not go all the way up the sides of a pie pan), keeping the thickness as uniform as possible. Place in refrigerator for at least 20 minutes to set.

Combine butter, remaining sweetener, remaining salt, and cream in a medium saucepan over medium heat. Bring to boil, then simmer. Cook until golden and syrup coats back of wooden spoon. Remove from heat and stir in extracts. Allow it to cool until the outside of the saucepan can be comfortably touched but is still warm, add in egg, stirring briskly as you combine it.

Retrieve pie crust from refrigerator. Place pecans in crust and pour sauce over it evenly. Cover edges of crust with foil. Bake about 30 minutes until filling is set. Cool completely before cutting and serving.

Keto Beignets

Servings: 8; Net Carbs: 5 g*; Calories: 697*; Fat: 65 g*; Protein: 13 g

- ✓ 3/4 cups lukewarm water
- ✓ 1/2 envelope (1-1/8 teaspoons) dry active yeast
- ✓ 1/4 cup xylitol or equivalent measurement of the zero carb sweetener of your choice
- ✓ 1 large egg, slightly beaten
- ✓ 1/2 teaspoon salt
- ✓ 1/2 cup heavy cream
- ✓ 4 cups almond flour
- ✓ 2 tablespoons coconut oil
- ✓ 1 cup peanut oil
- ✓ Non-stick cooking spray
- ✓ 1/2 cup xylitol or equivalent measurement of the zero carb sweetener of your choice, ground in a food processor until powdered sugar consistency

Combine water and yeast and allow to sit for 20 minutes.

Mix xylitol, eggs, salt, and heavy cream. Add to the yeast mixture. Then add 2 cups of flour and stir until well combined. Add coconut oil. Continue stirring while you add 1-1/2 more cups of flour. Sprinkle a little of the remaining flour on a flat surface, and gently knead dough. Spray a bowl with non-stick cooking spray. Place dough into bowl, cover with towel and let rise in a warm place 2 hours.

Pour processed sugar in a paper bag. Heat oil in small skillet on high heat until about 350 F.

Roll out dough, using reserve flour to lightly dust surfaces again. Cut dough into 16 squares and fry until golden brown. Drain on paper towel for a few seconds and toss in bag with sugar to coat.

*Carbs, calories, and fats are estimates, numbers will be slightly lower.

Keto Strawberry Shortcake

Servings: 12; Net Carbs: 5 g; Calories: 288; Fat: 26 g; Protein: 7 g

- ✓ 1/4 cup coconut milk
- ✓ 3 large egg
- ✓ 2-1/4 cups almond flour
- ✓ 1 teaspoon baking powder
- ✓ 1 tablespoon xylitol or equivalent measurement of the zero carb sweetener of your choice
- ✓ 1/4 teaspoon Kosher salt
- ✓ 3 tablespoons coconut oil
- ✓ 3 cups sliced strawberries
- ✓ 2 tablespoons xylitol or equivalent measurement of the zero carb sweetener of your choice
- ✓ 1 tablespoon lemon juice
- ✓ 1-1/2 cups heavy cream
- ✓ 2 tablespoons xylitol or equivalent measurement of the zero carb sweetener of your choice
- ✓ 1/2 teaspoon vanilla extract

Preheat oven to 375 F.

Whisk egg and milk together in a small bowl. Combine flour, powder, 1 tablespoon sweetener, and salt in a medium bowl. Cut coconut oil into flour mixture. Stir in cream mixture. Do not overwork.

Using a cookie scoop, drop 12 scoops onto a parchment covered cookie sheet, keeping each biscuit at least 2" away from other biscuits

Bake 15-18 minutes or until tops begin to brown and biscuit is set. Cool on sheet tray until room temperature.

Toss strawberries, 2 tablespoons sweetener, and lemon juice together. Whisk cream, 2 tablespoon sweetener, and vanilla together until whipped into soft peaks. Place 1/4 cup strawberry mixture on top of cooled biscuit and top with 2 tablespoons of whipped cream.

Keto Sweet Calas

Servings: 6; Net Carbs: 2 g; Calories: 400*; Fat: 38 g*; Protein: 3 g

- ✓ 2 cups grated zucchini, steamed and chilled
- ✓ 1 cup peanut oil
- ✓ 1/4 cup xylitol or equivalent measurement of the zero carb sweetener of your choice
- ✓ 2 teaspoons baking powder
- ✓ 1/4 teaspoon salt
- ✓ 1/4 teaspoon nutmeg
- ✓ 1/4 teaspoon cinnamon
- ✓ 4 teaspoons coconut flour
- ✓ 2 large eggs, beaten
- ✓ 1/4 teaspoon vanilla extract
- ✓ 1/4 cup xylitol or equivalent measurement of the zero carb sweetener of your choice, processed in a food processor until the consistency of powdered sugar.

Grate 2 cups zucchini. Steam covered in microwave on high until tender approximately 3-5 minutes. Place in large bowl in refrigerator to chill.

Heat peanut oil in Dutch oven over medium high heat.

Combine sweetener, baking powder, salt, nutmeg, cinnamon, and coconut flour in a small bowl.

Add eggs and vanilla into zucchini. Stir in baking powder mixture.

As soon as oil is hot (about 360 F), use a small ice cream scoop to scoop batter and release it into the oil. Do not cook more than 6 at a time to prevent overcrowding. Cook for approximately 3 minutes, flip each halfway through cooking.

When the calas are golden, remove from oil and place on paper towels to drain. Sprinkle with powdered sweetener.

ABOUT THE AUTHOR

Vonnie Lynn is a homemaker and mother who loves whipping up healthy and new recipes for her family in the kitchen. She is also an educator who has devoted 20 years of her life to teach special education. She loves teaching others and helping them improve their lives. By writing diet and self-help books, she hopes her readers learn to feel good about themselves as they improve their health and self-image. She chose to focus on the Keto diet because of its use in helping children with epilepsy have fewer seizures.

She currently lives in North Central Idaho with her husband, their two sons, two very spoiled dogs, and a cat. When she isn't researching her next book or trying out the latest recipe she has created on her family, she enjoys sitting on her porch swing and looking out at the scenic mountains and hiking. On the more frigid winter days, she enjoys cozying up with a book in front of the fire or doing jigsaw puzzles.

Made in the USA
Columbia, SC
10 November 2022